DAVE REAY studied Marine Biology at Liverpool University and graduated in 1994. He went on to gain a PhD with the British Antarctic Survey and Essex University, studying the effects of warming in the Southern Ocean. After gaining his doctorate he continued working as a post-doc at Essex, investigating the soil methane sink. In 2001 he moved to Edinburgh University to investigate greenhouse gas emissions from agriculture and forests, and went on to become a Natural Environment Research Council (NERC) Fellow in the School of Geosciences. Dave is now a lecturer in carbon management and director of

v MSc in Carbon
also the author
Begins at Home
r of GreenHouse
leading climate
site. Dave lives in
ife, two daughters
brador.

YOUR PLANET NEEDS YOU!

A Kids' Guide to Going Green

DAVE REAY

Illustrated by
ALAN ROWE

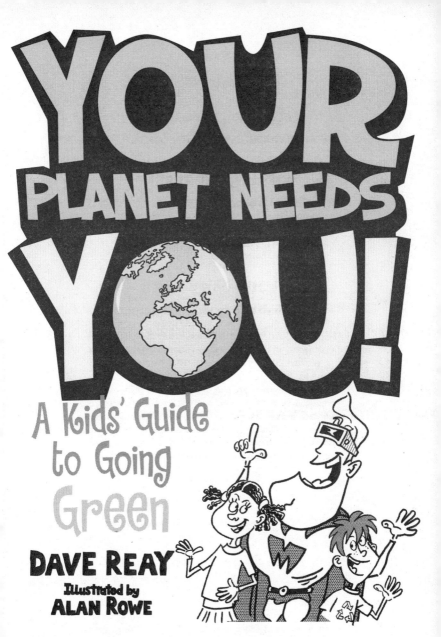

MACMILLAN CHILDREN'S BOOKS

For Maddy and Molly

First published 2009 by Macmillan Children's Books
a division of Macmillan Publishers Limited
20 New Wharf Road, London N1 9RR
Basingstoke and Oxford
Associated companies throughout the world
www.panmacmillan.com

ISBN 978-0-330-45095-9

Text copyright © Dave Reay 2009
Illustrations copyright © Alan Rowe 2009
With thanks to Leo Rowe-Brown for the Henry's Homework illustrations

The right of Dave Reay and Alan Rowe to be identified as the
author and illustrator of this work has been asserted by them in accordance
with the Copyright, Designs and Patents Act 1988.

1 3 5 7 9 8 6 4 2

A CIP catalogue record for this book is available from
the British Library.

Typeset by Nigel Hazle
Printed and bound in the UK by CPI Mackays, Chatham ME5 8TD

*T*hank you to my wife Sarah for providing all the best ideas. To my parents, brothers and sister for a childhood filled with the wonders of the outdoors. And to Sir David Attenborough for inspiring me and millions of others to better value and respect this world of which we are all part. Also huge thanks to Gaby Morgan and Rachel Petty, my editors at Macmillan, for expertly steering this book through some stormy seas, and to Alison Conboy and Chris Rapley at the Science Museum.

Are you ready to take on the greatest challenge to humankind of the twenty-first century? This challenge is not for the faint-hearted. Are you brave enough to command armies of rubbish-chomping worms, exterminate waste and explore the smelliest corners of the fridge? You'll become an expert in why cows have bad breath, why eating soup in Alaska is so dangerous and where to find the biggest ice lollies in the world. If you could be a climate champion, if you are ready to help fight this global battle, then . . .

YOUR PLANET NEEDS YOU!

Ever since the first hairy-backed caveman found that cooking mammoth meat on fires, rather than eating it raw, made it taste better, people have been changing the environment. For 200,000 years these effects were quite small: some tree-chopping here, some farming there and the occasional big fire when Caveman Og got a bit too carried away with his mammoth cooking and burned down the forest.

Then humans found coal, oil and gas – wonder-fuels made of the fossils of plants and animals that packed a real energy punch, and could be used for all sorts of brilliant things. Before too long modern-day Ogs were driving around in cars, flying in aeroplanes, lighting and heating their homes at the flick of a switch, and generally having a much nicer time than the original Og.

All this was great, but for one thing: the more of these fossil fuels people burned, the more the planet warmed up and the more weather patterns all over the world started to change.

 2

The problem is called climate change. And it's getting worse . . .

As the world gets warmer, more and more people and animals are being put in danger from the effects. The seas are rising and flooding more land and the stunning multicoloured beauty of tropical reefs is being replaced with large patches of dead white coral. From the highest mountains to the deepest jungles, climate change is a creeping threat that needs an army of champions to tackle it – an army of people

like you. So follow Max, Henry and Flora on their adventures around the world to see what is happening and what you can do to make a difference!

MAXIMUS – SAVIOUR OF WORLDS, CHAMPION FOR GOOD, PROTECTOR OF HUMANKIND AND CHOCOLATE FANATIC – IS HAVING A BAD NIGHT IN HIS TOP-SECRET ICE CAVE IN THE ANDES. IT'S TOO HOT AND THE DRIPPING OF THE MELTING ICE IS KEEPING HIM AWAKE.

In the far distance is another town and, as the sun begins to rise, Maximus heads on over.

'It certainly feels pretty warm here. Switch to heat vision. Now I can see the heat escaping from all the houses . . . Hang on, what's that?'

Tucked in among the rows and rows of glowing houses there is one that doesn't glow at all.

VERY ODD. THERE'S NO HEAT ESCAPING FROM THAT ONE. I THINK I'D BETTER INVESTIGATE.

The non-glowing house in question is number 24 Acacia Drive, home of Henry Hutchinson. It's Sunday morning and Henry is lying on his bed reading a comic. It's a really good comic and the massed armies of Grumph the Great are just getting ready to charge towards the castle walls of Hugrawn the Horrid.

Out of the corner of his eye Henry sees a shadow pass his window. Now, it could have been his imagination, but he's sure he saw a person out there. This is weird because his bedroom window is five metres above the ground.

Carefully, Henry tiptoes to the window and with a quick tug pulls the curtain back. Hovering outside, and looking rather embarrassed, is Maximus.

Faster than a speeding bullet Maximus hides behind the nearest lamp post.

At Climate Club, Henry introduces Max to his
best friend, Flora, who is busy making a poster.

'Max, this is Flora. She knows loads about
climate change.'

'Hi, Max,' says Flora, looking up from her
poster. 'I like your tights. So, do you want to be a
climate champion too? We can always use more
help.'

'Er . . . yes, I think so. But I don't know much
about it.'

'Don't worry. Miss Weatherbottom is really

 12

good and I can tell you loads of stuff as well if you like.'

Henry points at a grumpy-looking boy standing in the corner picking his nose.

'That's Gripper Jenkins. He's only here because he's on detention.'

They stop chatting as Miss Weatherbottom sweeps into the room.

'Hello, Climate Clubbers!' she says. 'I see there are some new faces here today. Now, I recognize Gripper – do stop picking your nose, Gripper.' She turns to Max, who has squeezed into a chair that is far too small for his superhero bottom.

'And you are?'

Max stands up, but the chair comes with him. 'I am Maximus, Saviour of Worlds, Champion for Good, Protector of Humankind and Chocolate Fanatic. But you can call me Max.'

'Then hello, Max, and welcome! Right, first of all, well done, Henry, for your excellent homework from last week. It was so good I've made a copy for everyone.'

Henry Hutchinson

In your own words, describe what climate change is.

The whole planet is warming up. And the warmer it gets the more the weather all round the world is changing. That means that cold places aren't as cold any more and dry places are even drier.

Whenever we use electricity, drive cars or go on aeroplanes we add more and more gases to the air. These gases are called 'greenhouse gases' and they're special because they can trap heat. The greenhouse gas that humans add most of to the atmosphere is called **carbon dioxide** and there's now so much of it up there trapping heat that it's making the whole planet warmer.

boom!

HPOLLUT

spulter

Reading Henry's homework, Max is beginning to understand the problem. 'So climate change is the same as global warming?' he asks.

'People often use the words to describe the same thing, Max,' says Miss Weatherbottom, 'but an easy way to think of it is that the world is warming up – which is global warming – and this increase in temperature is in turn changing the patterns of weather – climate change. So climate change is caused by global warming. And the reason the world is heating up is because we are adding more of these heat-trapping gases – called greenhouse gases – to the air.'

Gripper puts up his hand. 'Miss, my uncle's got a greenhouse and it gets really hot inside. Is that bad?'

'No, Gripper, but the reason it gets hot does help explain the extra warming we're seeing around the whole planet. As the sun shines down on your uncle's greenhouse it heats up the air inside, but the glass keeps the heat from escaping. The gases that cause global warming act like the glass, keeping the heat from escaping from our planet and into space. That's why they're called greenhouse gases.'

Gripper's hand shoots up again. 'Miss, my uncle's got a big car with a button you can press that says Climate Control. Does that mean he can control global warming?'

'I'm afraid not,' Miss Weatherbottom explains. 'In fact big cars are one of the big problems. They produce a lot of the greenhouse gas called carbon dioxide and so can give you a really big carbon footprint.'

'Er . . . I'm a size six, miss. I don't know how big my uncle's feet are, but they're very smelly.'

Miss Weatherbottom laughs. 'No, Gripper! Your carbon footprint isn't about how big your feet are. It's about the amount of greenhouse gases each person is responsible for. Someone who travels in a big car and wastes lots of electricity at home can produce enough greenhouse gases to fill ten houses each year and will have a really big carbon footprint.'

'I get it,' says Henry. 'So to make your carbon footprint smaller you need to cut down on the greenhouse gases you produce, like by saving energy at home.'

'That's right, Henry. And that's your challenge for today's homework. I want each of you to draw a picture of your house and make a list of the ways you can make your own carbon footprint smaller at home. The best one wins a special climate-champion prize.'

'Do ice caves count?' asks Max.

'Absolutely, Max. No doubt Flora and Henry will be able to help you. See you all tomorrow.'

Max, Henry and Flora head for the school gate.

Max looks confused. 'I think I understand a bit more about these heat-trapping gases that are causing the problem,' he says, 'but how come I've never seen them?'

'They're invisible,' replies Flora. 'If we could fly as high as a jet plane, I could show you.'

'No problem,' says Max, swishing his cape. 'Hold on to my arms, you two . . . and off we go!'

WHOA! WE CAN SEE FOR MILES UP HERE, MAX!

ONE OF THE PERKS OF HANGING OUT WITH A SUPERHERO!

SO, IF THESE GASES ARE INVISIBLE, HOW AM I SUPPOSED TO SEE THEM?

THEY'RE ALL AROUND US. THE AIR'S A BIG MIXTURE OF DIFFERENT GASES. SOME OF THEM, LIKE OXYGEN, DON'T TRAP ANY HEAT – THOUGH IT'S PRETTY HANDY FOR BREATHING – AND ALTHOUGH GREENHOUSE GASES LIKE CARBON DIOXIDE ARE ONLY A TINY PART OF THE MIXTURE, THEY'RE SO GOOD AT TRAPPING HEAT THAT TOGETHER THEY KEEP THE EARTH WARM.

WEIRD. IT FEELS COOLER UP HERE THAN DOWN ON THE GROUND.

IT SHOULD. WE'RE SO HIGH UP THAT THE GREENHOUSE GASES HAVE TRAPPED A LOT OF THE HEAT COMING FROM THE EARTH BEFORE IT GETS TO US. MAYBE YOU CAN SEE THEM – HAVE YOU GOT SUPER-VISION?

Bouncing beams

So how does global warming actually work?
Well, it's really all down to the Sun, bouncing
around energy and greenhouse gases. Of all the
energy the Sun beams towards Earth about a
third is reflected straight back into space by
our atmosphere. The rest heads on down to
the ground, but even there a lot of it is bounced
straight back towards space, especially when it
hits very reflective surfaces like snow. It's when
the Sun's energy hits darker surfaces that things
really start to hot up. Dark surfaces absorb a lot
of the energy and warm up. This is why black
surfaces like roads get really hot on a sunny day
while white surfaces stay cooler.

The heat from our planet's surface heads
back towards space too, but it is this form of
energy that the greenhouse gases can trap. It's
a good thing they do, because without them the
average temperature on our planet would be a

rather chilly -18°C. The greenhouse gases trap enough of the heat energy coming up from the Earth's surface to keep the average temperature of the planet at a rather more comfortable 14°C. But here's the problem. The more we add to the amounts of greenhouse gases in the atmosphere the more heat energy is trapped, and so the more our planet heats up – in the last 100 years it has increased by almost 1°C. So although the greenhouse effect by itself is a good thing, it's the extra global warming caused by us that's the big worry.

Max sighs. 'Hmm, it all still seems a bit complicated. My brain's starting to hurt and all this talk of global warming is making me hot.'

'No problem, Max,' says Henry. 'I've got a picture of how global warming works here in my school bag. If we really want to see it all in action we need to fly on towards the North Pole – that should cool you down a bit!'

Henry Hutchinson

Draw a diagram of the Earth to show what happens to solar energy, greenhouse gases and the energy radiating from Earth.

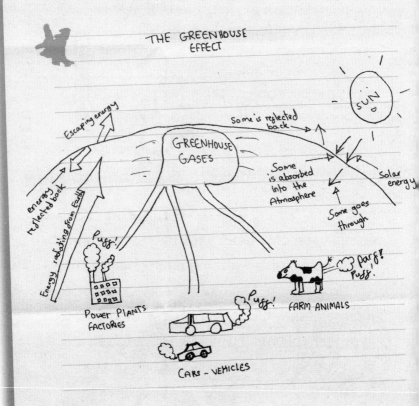

THE GREENHOUSE EFFECT

SUN

Escaping energy

Some is reflected back

GREENHOUSE GASES

Some is absorbed into the Atmosphere

energy reflected back

Solar energy

Some goes through

Energy radiating from Earth

Puff!

Power Plants Factories

Puff!

Parp! Puff!

FARM ANIMALS

CARS - VEHICLES

The greenhouse gases trap a lot of the energy Earth radiates out towards space. So the more gases, the hotter it is.

Main greenhouse gases

- Carbon dioxide from fossil fuels and deforestation
- Methane, which comes from farm animals
- Nitrous oxide from fields and vehicles

Well done, Henry! What enormous cows!

B

CHAPTER THREE

28

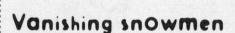

Vanishing snowmen

The hotter the Earth gets, the less snow and ice we have. This means that our planet becomes less and less white and therefore less reflective – so less of the Sun's energy is reflected back into space, and more is absorbed by the ground and turned into heat energy. This warms up the planet even more, which leads to even less snow and ice …

'So let me see if I've got this right,' says Max. 'Light-coloured stuff like snow reflects heat and light, but dark stuff like rocks and grass absorb it. That makes sense – I once sat down on a black chair in the President's garden on a really hot day and nearly melted my tights.

I don't think he was very impressed when I had to run and sit in the fountain to cool down.'

'That's funny!' laughs Henry. 'But you're right. I invented a great experiment to demonstrate this for Miss Weatherbottom's class last year. For some reason she didn't like it much. It goes like this.'

Henry Hutchinson

Design an experiment to demonstrate the way that different colours reflect or absorb heat.

Wait for a really sunny day when your mum and dad are sunbathing. Find two old plastic bottles. Paint one white and one black and let them dry. Now fill them both with ice-cold water and put them in a very sunny place. Leave them for about an hour. Find your sunbathing relatives and pour the water from the black bottle over one of them, and the water from the white bottle over the other one. Compare how much they scream

ice-cold water

Sunny day

white →

← black

when the water from each bottle hits them.
The water in the black bottle should be nice
and warm because dark things are so good
at trapping heat energy from the Sun. The
water in the white bottle will probably feel quite
cold — and so produce the louder scream —
because white is good at reflecting the Sun's
energy.

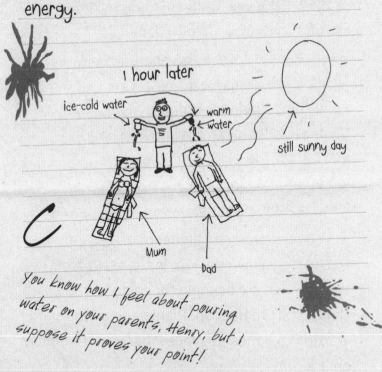

I hour later

ice-cold water

warm
water

still sunny day

Mum

Dad

You know how I feel about pouring
water on your parents, Henry, but I
suppose it proves your point!

Max, Henry and Flora have landed on an iceberg in the Arctic Ocean.

'He looks hungry,' whispers Max nervously.

'He probably is,' says Henry. 'Miss Weatherbottom said that as the ice melts polar bears are finding it much harder to hunt for food.'

Max looks worried. 'Poor polar bear. So, animals are affected by global warming too?' he asks. 'I hadn't thought of that.'

'Yeah,' says Flora sadly, 'loads of them. Some animals that like to live on mountains are going higher and higher up to escape the warming lower down. In the sea, some types of fish are heading for colder waters as things start to heat up. Plants and animals are starting to appear in places that used to be too cold for them.'

Max cheers up a bit. 'That could be quite exciting! I mean, you could end up with a banana plant in your back garden. Then you could make some yummy milkshakes!'

'It would be fun,' Flora agrees, 'but if the climate changes too quickly a lot of the plants and animals won't be able to move fast enough. Loads could die out entirely.'

'That's terrible! I mean, it's not even their fault. There must be something I can do to help.' Max thinks hard. 'OK, lifting whole forests up would be tricky, but I could start flying some of the animals to colder places, maybe give a few birds a helping hand if they need it . . .'

'I'm sorry, Max,' says Flora, 'but even if you could move them all – and there are billions of them – there just isn't anywhere to put most of them. They each rely on a whole network of other animals and plants for their food and shelter, and unless they have all this in the new place too they probably won't survive.'

The climate escalator

More and more animals and plants are responding to a warming planet and the changes in weather patterns that this causes. Some types of bird are changing the place they migrate to and going at a different time of year. Other animals and plants are retreating from the hotter temperatures near the Earth's equator and spreading towards the cool of the North and South Poles. For the many animals and plants that live on mountains, escaping a hotter climate means moving higher and higher up, like riding on a slow-moving climate escalator.

In the high mountains of Spain there is a beautiful butterfly that is fast retreating upwards. The black-veined butterfly has already been pushed 300 metres further up the mountains it lives on – if its eggs are brought back down to the places it used to live in they all die.

From furry guinea-pig-like animals called pika getting too hot on the mountains of America to the trees in Siberia spreading further and further north, changes in climate are affecting

billions of animals and plants. By the middle of this century climate change could mean that one out of every three plant and animal species on the land will be set on the road to extinction.

'I think we might be on the extinction list too if we don't get away from this polar bear,' says Max nervously. 'C'mon, let's head back to Henry's house and have some chocolate to calm our nerves!'

CHAPTER
FOUR

BACK HOME, MAX, HENRY AND FLORA ARE ENJOYING DOUBLE CHOC CHIP SUNDAES IN THE GARDEN.

RIGHT, I THINK I'VE GOT IT – MORE OF THESE GREENHOUSE GASES ARE CAUSING THE PLANET TO WARM UP AND THREATENING LOADS OF ANIMALS, INCLUDING US. SO ALL I HAVE TO DO TO SAVE THE WORLD IS COLLECT THE GASES UP – IN A GIANT BALLOON OR SOMETHING – AND THROW THEM OUT INTO SPACE.

I'M NOT SURE . . . THERE ARE QUITE A LOT OF GREENHOUSE GASES ALREADY UP THERE, MAX, ESPECIALLY CARBON DIOXIDE.

HOW MUCH ARE WE TALKING? TEN TONNES? TWENTY TONNES? I DO HAVE SUPER-STRENGTH, YOU KNOW.

WELL, EVERY YEAR PEOPLE ADD ABOUT ANOTHER TWENTY-FIVE THOUSAND MILLION TONNES TO OUR ATMOSPHERE.

OH, I SEE WHAT YOU MEAN. THAT'S QUITE A LOT . . .

38

Water bomb

The most important greenhouse gas in our atmosphere is actually **water vapour**. There are billions of tonnes floating around up there, with a constant cycle of it forming into the droplets that make up clouds, falling back to Earth as rain and snow, and then evaporating into the air as water vapour again. The most worrying greenhouse gas that humans add to the atmosphere is **carbon dioxide**, which we mainly produce by burning fossil fuels like oil, gas and coal. The other big ones are **methane**, which comes from cows, rubbish tips and really wet soils like rice paddies, and **nitrous oxide**, which is also known as laughing gas and mostly comes from fields where farmers have added lots of fertilizer.

By adding all these greenhouse gases to the atmosphere we warm it up a bit. The warmer the air gets the more water vapour it can hold and as water vapour is a powerful greenhouse gas too, the atmosphere then gets even warmer. Scientists call this a '**feedback**'.

Max realizes that he is going to have to find out a bit more about the causes of global warming before he can go about saving the planet.

'I'm going to have a closer look at this carbon dioxide stuff Flora was talking about,' he says, switching to Super-vision. 'Ooh, there's loads coming out of that chimney there – and, wait, you're breathing it out too! And so am I! Does breathing add to global warming?'

'Well, not really,' replies Henry. 'There's this huge balance between all the living things breathing carbon dioxide out and the plants, soils and oceans taking it back up and storing it. And . . . Max, you're turning blue!'

'MAX!' shouts Henry. 'Breathing isn't the problem.'

Flora smiles. 'Seriously – it's OK for us to breathe. Like Henry was saying, plants and the oceans take up the carbon dioxide that humans and other life forms breathe out. It's the extra gas produced from burning fossil fuels that's the real problem.'

Max exhales loudly. 'So we breathe it out and the plants take it in. Hey, how about if we had loads more trees then? They could take up the extra stuff that comes from cars and factories.'

'It's a great idea, Max,' says Flora, 'but we'd need an awful lot more trees and at the moment many of the big forests are actually being cut down.'

'What! That will make the problem even worse, won't it? Come on, show me where this is going on.'

What's that smell?

The greenhouse gases are all good at trapping heat energy, but some are better at it than others. Water vapour and carbon dioxide are the two most important because there is so much of them in our atmosphere, but other greenhouse gases like methane (from cow burps and farts) and nitrous oxide (from farmers' fields) are very good at trapping heat energy even though there's much less of them. One balloon full of methane released into the air can warm the planet as much as ten balloons full of carbon dioxide. Nitrous oxide is even more powerful, one balloon's worth causing as much warming as 300 balloons full of carbon dioxide.

Henry Hutchinson

Identify three greenhouse gases
and how they are produced:

Carbon dioxide
Big Sources:
Cars, trucks and planes
Cement factories and power stations
Heating, lighting and appliances

trapped
heat
energy

parp!

parp!

Methane
Big Sources:
Rice fields
Stinky landfill sites
Burping and farting cows and manure

parp!

Parp!

Nitrous oxide
Big Sources:
Farms and fertilizer
Power stations and factories
Cars

Methane

*A very good, Henry, but I do wish
you wouldn't use the word 'fart'.*

Flora's facts

The average person emits just a few litres of methane per month, but a cow can burp and fart out 500 litres in a day!

CHAPTER
FIVE

Max, Henry and Flora land on the edge of the tall rainforest. On one side is the deep dark green of the trees, on the other are barren soils stretching away into the distance.

'I think this is what happens when all the trees are cut down,' Henry tells Max. 'The land gets used for growing food for a bit and then when the soil is no longer any good another chunk of forest is cut down.'

'But if it keeps on like this the forest will disappear!' says Max, alarmed.

'I know. It's a really big problem. People want the trees for firewood and to make houses and furniture and they need the land to grow more food, but the more forest we lose the fewer trees there are to soak up all the carbon dioxide we're adding to the air.'

Henry Hutchinson

Describe the importance of plants and trees in maintaining a stable climate.

When plants grow on land or in the sea they use carbon dioxide. In a forest a lot of this then gets turned into the wood in the trunks and branches of the trees, staying locked away from causing global warming for years and years. Even small plants and the tiny ones in the sea do their bit because when they die some of the carbon in them is stored away in the soil or in deep ocean mud. Altogether these stores for carbon dioxide — called **carbon sinks** — mop up about half of the stuff

we produce from burning fossil fuels like coal and oil every year. Without them we'd be in really big trouble, but they just can't keep up.

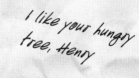

Tree absorbing carbon dioxide (CO_2)

yum yum

A

I like your hungry tree, Henry

Max is thinking hard. 'So the bits of the world that trap the greenhouse gases are getting smaller while the amount that comes from cars and everything is getting bigger? That can't be good.'

'No, it isn't,' says Henry. 'That's why we need everyone to start cutting down on the energy they waste instead of cutting down more trees. Though I know Flora thinks it's up to people like the President to change things.'

Flora shakes her head. 'I just don't think people like us can do much. I mean, I do my best, but there are billions of people in the world. What difference will it make if only the three of us make our carbon footprints smaller?'

'Hmm. But, then again, if all those billions of people each did a small bit . . .'

'Maybe you're right, Henry. Anyway, Max, how's your head feeling now?' asks Flora. 'Do you see how global warming works?'

Max is still a little confused. 'I understand why global warming is happening and why it's

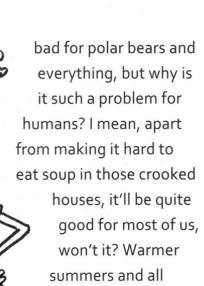

bad for polar bears and everything, but why is it such a problem for humans? I mean, apart from making it hard to eat soup in those crooked houses, it'll be quite good for most of us, won't it? Warmer summers and all that?'

'The trouble is that climate change isn't just about more sunny days – people all over the world are beginning to suffer from its effects,' explains Henry.

Max chuckles. 'What, like sweaty armpits and stuff? Could get quite smelly, I'll admit.'

'More B.O. is the least of our problems,' says Flora. 'First of all there's the rising

sea level – as the oceans heat up the water expands, so the sea gets higher. On top of that there's all the extra water being added to the sea from the melting ice.'

'Hmm, that would explain all the puddles in my ice cave. But surely people can build higher sea walls or move uphill if things get difficult?' asks Max, confident that he has solved the problem.

'That's possible for some of us,' says Henry,

'but there are lots of places where there isn't enough money to build sea walls – or any hills to escape to. Some people are already having to abandon their homes. If you give us another lift, we'll show you.'

Grandpa Greenhouse

Shivering at his desk in nineteenth-century Stockholm, a Swedish scientist called Svante Arrhenius had warmer times on his mind. He knew that all over the world people were burning more and more coal, which meant that

more and more of the greenhouse gas called carbon dioxide was being released. Arrhenius worked out that if you doubled the amount of carbon dioxide in the air the planet would, on average, warm up by about 5°C. He was quite pleased with this, as his toes were beginning to go numb. But he reckoned it would take about 3,000 years to happen, so he just had to put on an extra pair of socks. Arrhenius was right about more carbon dioxide warming up the planet, but wrong about how long it would take for the amount of it in the air to increase. Instead of taking 3,000 years, it's now predicted to double in less than 200! As a result, scientists predict that the planet will warm by between 1°C and 6°C during this century.

CHAPTER
SIX

THIS TIME KEEP AN EYE OUT FOR A PLACE WITH LOADS OF RIVERS. THIS IS BANGLADESH, SO WE'VE COME TO THE RIGHT PLACE. THE WATER LEVEL HERE IS RISING AND PEOPLE ARE HAVING TO LEAVE THEIR HOMES.

I CAN SEE SOME RIVERS DOWN THERE. THEY'RE MASSIVE AND THEY WIND ALONG LIKE SNAKES.

THAT'S THE PLACE. FLY US DOWN TO THAT VILLAGE THERE AND LET'S TAKE A CLOSER LOOK.

Henry, Flora and Max make a splash landing among some mangrove trees, and are instantly up to their knees in a flood.

'C'mon,' says Henry. 'Let's head over to that house and get out of this water.'

Henry Hutchinson

Describe why climate change leads to sea levels rising.

The seas get higher as our planet warms up for two main reasons. First of all, as the water in the sea gets warmer it expands and takes up more and more space. The other reason is loads of melting ice. If the ice is already floating in the sea, then it doesn't change the sea level when it melts. But if the ice is on land it can have a big effect if it melts.

$A+$

Excellent idea, Henry, with very nice drawings. Well done!

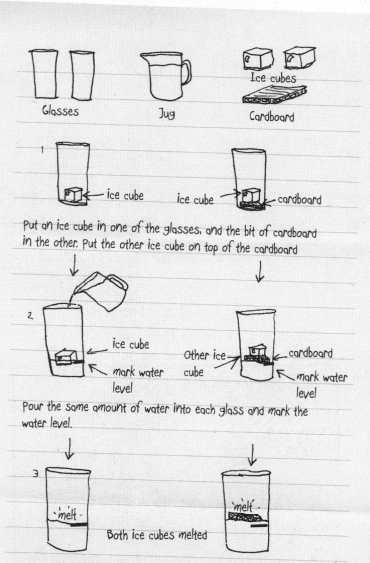

Glasses   Jug   Ice cubes

Cardboard

1

ice cube   ice cube   cardboard

Put an ice cube in one of the glasses, and the bit of cardboard in the other. Put the other ice cube on top of the cardboard

2

ice cube

mark water level

Other ice cube   cardboard

mark water level

Pour the same amount of water into each glass and mark the water level.

3

melt   melt

Both ice cubes melted

When the ice cubes have melted, the water level in the glass with the cardboard raft in it will be higher.

Max, Henry and Flora arrive at the veranda of a house surrounded by the flood, where a girl sits dangling her feet in the water.

The gang introduce themselves. 'We're

here because we'd like to find out more about global warming,' explains Max.

'I'm Shirin,' the girl replies, 'and you've come to the right place. Our village is being flooded all the time. We try to keep the water out by building mud walls and ditches, but it always finds a way in. The water is just getting too high for us to carry on living here. That bit over there used to be our vegetable garden, but all the plants have died because the sea keeps flooding in. We can't move uphill because there's nowhere higher to go. Mum and Dad say we have to abandon our house and move to a new part of the country, far away from the rivers and the sea – lots of my friends have left already. It's really sad, but I don't think people in other countries know what's happening to us . . .'

'Well, it's about time they did,' says Max. 'I thought the flooding in my ice cave was bad, but this is terrible.'

'That's why we need the President and leaders of all the rich countries to do more,' says Flora. 'Most of the greenhouse gases that cause the problem are from countries like mine where we have lots of money to build new sea walls and protect people. But it's people like Shirin with a tiny carbon footprint who are suffering from climate change the most.'

Excuse my big feet

A carbon footprint is the amount of greenhouse gases a person is responsible for producing each year. In developed countries where people use a lot of electricity, drive big cars and fly in planes a lot, most carbon footprints are really big. Also, they've been producing carbon emissions for longer. In less developed countries, people's carbon footprints are much smaller, as they are just catching up with us in terms of industry, but these countries are often the ones most in danger from climate change because of where

they are geographically. Many of their leaders
think that this is really unfair and that the
people in rich nations with their big carbon
footprints should do more to help protect
the people in poorer countries from climate
change. It's also important that we help them
to develop without making the same
mistakes we have, by investing in
greener technologies.

CHAPTER SEVEN

The three friends say goodbye to Shirin and leave the waterlogged village.

'Poor Shirin,' says Henry as they soar off into the skies. 'I can't believe that she's losing her home, and that millions of other people around the world are at risk of the same thing.'

'I know, it's terrible,' replies Max. 'But surely there can't be *millions* like her. I mean, hers is only a very small village, after all.'

'It's not just one village, Max,' says Flora. 'Many millions of people all around the world live close to the sea or a big river. Add things like hurricanes and torrential rainstorms to the fact that the sea is creeping higher and higher and you've got one enormous flooding problem.'

'Hang on a minute – we've got things like hurricanes and rainstorms already. What have they got to do with global warming?'

'I should have said. As the planet warms up it alters the normal patterns of weather around the world. This is what scientists call "climate change".'

Henry Hutchinson

Explain the difference between weather, climate and climate change.

Weather and climate are not the same thing. Weather is what's happening outside at the moment. Hot or cold, sunny or rainy — it's all still weather.

Climate describes what the average weather is like in your area over many years. That means that if you live in a place with a hot and dry climate there might be a lot of days when it's sunny, but you'll still get rainy weather now and again. Bad weather in a nice climate is a bit like having the best school dinner lady in the world: the food on most days is really nice, but now and again she still serves Brussels sprouts.

Climate change is where the normal weather patterns in an area (the climate) starts to misbehave. The winters might start getting much warmer than usual, or there might be more sunny days over the summer holidays than there used to be. Some changes in climate might seem nice, but others are definitely more like sprouts.

B Sprouts are actually very good for you, Henry, but I see what you mean!

'Aha!' says Max. 'Now I understand why everyone keeps talking about global warming *and* climate change. Global warming is the world getting warmer and it's this extra warming that causes climate change.'

'You've got it, Max,' says Henry. 'And we're likely to see some damaging types of weather, like heatwaves, becoming more common. Massive storms like hurricanes draw their power from the sea, and the warmer the water

at the surface is the more
powerful they can become.'

'Even more powerful
hurricanes! Now, I
know that's not
good – I flew
near one once
and it nearly
sucked my
boots off.'

'Yeah, they can
do massive amounts of damage to houses
and so can the really torrential rainstorms
we're likely to see more of. A lot of towns and
cities just aren't ready for so much extra water
pouring down on them all in one go.'

'Talking of flooding, my cape is feeling
pretty soggy after our visit to Shirin's village.
Can we find somewhere to go and dry off
now?'

'Yes,' agrees Henry. 'Let's go and check out
climate change in the desert.'

'Er . . . is climate change a problem in

deserts too?' asks Max, wrinkling his brow. 'I mean, more rain is just what they need, isn't it? And surely they can't get much hotter?'

'The problem is the different ways global warming is changing the climate around the world,' replies Flora. 'In some places the average weather will get much wetter, but a lot of places that are already short of rain will get drier and drier. Come on, fly us down to Australia. They've got some massive deserts there and we might even see some kangaroos!'

WhOdunnit?

There was plenty of dangerous weather like hurricanes around long before humans started to change the climate. When we have a really bad storm, a deadly heatwave or torrential rains that flood houses it's almost impossible for scientists to say whether these events have been caused by global warming or would have happened anyway. What we do know is that these types of damaging weather are likely to get even more damaging and happen even more often as the planet warms up.

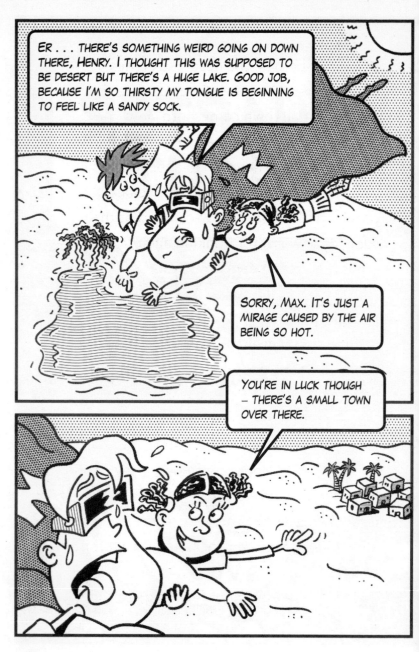

Below our heroes, the desert stretches out for miles in every direction. Swept by the shifting sands, a small town comes into view.

As the trio comes to a sandy crash landing, Flora explains. 'They've had a really bad few years here. It's always been a dry place, but they've had so little rain recently that the supplies of water for drinking and growing crops are getting dangerously low.'

'Hope they can spare a glassful for me,' remarks Max.

'Er . . . they probably can, Max. But it's recycled water, you know,' Flora warns him.

'What? You can recycle water?' says Max. 'I thought that was for things like paper and cans. How do they recycle water?'

'Well, Max,' Henry continues, 'they clean up things like old washing-up water and reuse it, but in places like this they have to recycle all the water they can, including the stuff from toilets.'

'Ah. I'm suddenly not feeling quite so thirsty.'

From flood to thirst

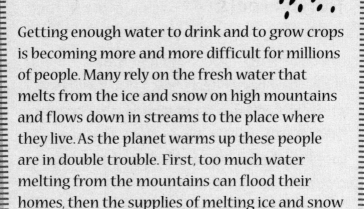

Getting enough water to drink and to grow crops is becoming more and more difficult for millions of people. Many rely on the fresh water that melts from the ice and snow on high mountains and flows down in streams to the place where they live. As the planet warms up these people are in double trouble. First, too much water melting from the mountains can flood their homes, then the supplies of melting ice and snow will start to run out and so the streams will dry up.

In very dry parts of the world like the Australian deserts, water supplies have already got so low that people have had to start recycling any water they have. They reuse the water from washing up and baths and, when things get really bad, they even recycle the water from toilets. Drinking water that's come from toilets, even after it has been cleaned up, isn't very popular, but many people now have no choice.

'So, let me get this straight,' says Max. ' In some places, like Shirin's home, there's far too much water, and in other places, like this, there's not nearly enough.'

'That's right. The changes in weather patterns that global warming causes mean that some places get much heavier rain and have more flooding, while others get much drier. We've even had water shortages at home this summer,' says Henry. 'Dad's not allowed to use the hosepipe to water the garden. But in other countries where it's even drier, things are much worse. It's getting harder and harder for people to find clean drinking water and the soils get too dry for farmers to grow their crops. The changes in climate that come from global warming could mean millions of people go hungry.'

Max sighs. 'We've got so much work to do, haven't we? Let's get out of here. We can stop off for a drink of water at my ice cave instead – there are plenty of ice cubes too if you want some!'

79

'Well, I suppose not everyone has been blessed with special flying powers, so they don't really have a choice,' replies Max, looking smug.

'But that's the thing, Max – they do!' says Henry. 'A lot of people on this plane will be flying back from their holidays, but they could have gone somewhere closer to home.'

Max thinks hard. 'I know,' he says. 'I can carry all the planes to their destinations using my SUPER STRENGTH!'

'Er . . . there are thousands of flights a day. I think a better answer would be for people to use trains whenever they can – they don't produce as much greenhouse gas as planes – and only take the plane when there's no other option.'

'Oh well.' Max sighs. 'Given the look of those lunches, they'll probably start doing that anyway.'

 80

Henry Hutchinson

Describe the different types of transport used for going on holiday and their climate-changing emissions.

Plane

Thanks to planes we can now travel further away from home than ever before. This is great, but it means we're pumping out lots of greenhouse gases. And planes fly high up in the air, where some of their emissions have a more powerful effect on climate change. So if we can't stop flying altogether I think we should at least ditch short-haul flights and save up flying for really important trips.

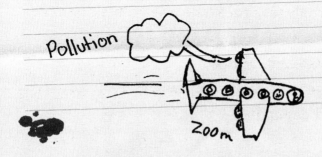

Pollution

Zoom

Car

Some cars are better than others (even without Dad's singing). If it's a big-engined gas guzzler then it could well prove to be a big producer of greenhouse gases too.

Train

Holidaying by train can be tricky with all those beach balls/skis/tennis racquets to carry. But if you and your family like to travel light then this wins hands down.

Well done, Henry! I suggest buying some earplugs to block out that singing!

CHAPTER
NINE

AS OUR HEROES SWOOP DOWN TOWARDS THE ICE-COVERED PEAKS OF THE ANDES THAT ARE HOME TO MAX, THE WIND IS WHISTLING AND BLOWING THE SNOW ACROSS A GIANT GLACIER.

OK. I GET THAT CLIMATE CHANGE IS REALLY DANGEROUS AND THAT GREENHOUSE GASES CAN CAUSE GLOBAL WARMING. BUT HOW DO WE KNOW IT'S REALLY THEIR FAULT? I MEAN, DO WE KNOW FOR SURE THAT THERE ARE MORE OF THEM NOW THAN THERE USED TO BE?

85

'See that gap in the ice, Max?' says Henry. 'There's a rope going down into it. Let's fly in and see what's going on.'

In the shelter of the ice cave all is quiet. The light shines blue through the ice, and there is the constant sound of dripping.

Max wraps himself in his cape. 'Pretty cold in here, isn't it?'

'Yes, freezing,' Henry agrees. 'Hey, look at the ice – it's full of those little bubbles I was telling you about. The ice near the top is the youngest, and the deeper down you go the older it gets. The bubbles down at the bottom there have got air in them from thousands of years ago. The rope goes all the way down. Let's go and have a look. OK, Max? MAX?' Max is licking the ice and his tongue is firmly stuck.

ERGH. HI HEEM HOO HAVE GOTH NY HONGUE THUCK.

'Ow, that hurt! It didn't taste very good either,' moans Max, freeing himself.

The three of them finally make it to the bottom of the cave, where they find a man with an ice pick breaking off chunks of ice.

HELLO, I'M DR DAVE. GLAD YOU THREE ARE HERE. I COULD DO WITH SOME HELP WITH THESE ICE CHUNKS.

Are you a scientist?' asks Flora.

'That's right. I'm collecting ice to measure the greenhouse gases in it. The bubbles down here were trapped about ten thousand years ago,' explains Dr Dave. 'Back then there was a lot less of each of the greenhouse gases in the air. But up near the top, in bubbles less than two hundred years old, you start to find much more because of more factories, cars and planes adding greenhouse gases to the atmosphere.'

'Ick! Frozen pollution!' says Max. 'No wonder my giant ice lolly didn't taste very nice!'

'People really started to produce a lot of greenhouse gases when they began burning coal, and later oil and gas,' explains Dr Dave. 'These are called fossil fuels, because they are made from the fossilized remains of plants and animals that died millions of years ago. Oil was formed from tiny plants and animals that lived, and then died, in prehistoric oceans. Coal is made mostly from plants that grew in swampy areas on the land.'

Max is amazed. 'So, coal and oil were made from loads of dead bodies?'

'Yes. It took millions of years to make them, deep under the land and sea, but now people are burning their way through about a million years' worth every single year to provide all the electricity we use, heat all the buildings, and fuel all the planes, trains and trucks. If we keep using oil at this rate, sooner or later we'll run out of it for cars and everything else,' explains Dr Dave.

'Hmm. That'll be good, won't it?' asks Max. 'I mean, if all these fossil fuels start to run out, there'll be less greenhouse gases getting chucked into the air.'

'If we wait until then before we do anything, we'll have already added too much greenhouse gas to the atmosphere to prevent really rapid global warming. C'mon, give me a hand to get these ice chunks back to my camp and I'll tell you more about it.'

Ice lolly time machines

Drilling a two-mile-long ice lolly isn't easy. Every few metres of ice has to be taken out carefully and the really deep stuff can be under so much pressure that it explodes when it gets to the surface. Once they have their giant ice lolly out safely, the scientists use special machines that are able to 'sniff' the air bubbles in the ice and so tell them about how the amount of greenhouse gases in the air has changed through history.

There is more greenhouse gas in the air bubbles the closer you get to the present. To power inventions like electric lighting, motor cars and refrigerators we've burned more and more fossil fuels and whenever these are burned more greenhouse gases are released into our atmosphere.

CHAPTER TEN

'They sound brilliant,' says Max. 'Imagine making your own electricity!'

'Yeah, there are more and more of them about. See that big square attached to the roof of Flora's house on the other side of our street?'

'I thought it was just a big window,' says Max. 'What's it for?'

'That's our solar panel,' replies Flora proudly. 'It makes electricity from the energy coming down from the Sun. On really sunny days it can give us all the electricity we need.'

'Hmm, not so good at night, I suppose . . .'

'No, but we do have a windmill too. So if it's windy we still get some electricity. Sometimes we make so much we can even send some back down the electricity lines and get paid for it.'

'Whoa! So Flora's house is like a little climate-change-fighting power station all by itself! I think you might have lost the carbon footprint competition, Henry.'

'Yes, Flora's house is good. But I'm not beaten yet. One of the best ways to stop all the power stations producing so much greenhouse gas is to use less electricity in the first place. Come on, I'll show you.'

Clean energy

Most of the energy we use for electricity and heating our homes comes from fossil fuels like coal and oil, and this means lots of greenhouse gases are produced.

But there are several other sources of energy that don't release as much greenhouse gases, and that won't run out like coal and oil will. These are called **renewables**. Most renewable energy is provided by the Sun, the wind and water. The Sun's energy is captured by **solar panels** that can either turn it into electricity or warm up water for houses. Wind energy is mostly obtained from giant windmills that make electricity as the wind turns their blades and drives the turbines inside them. Most of the energy we get from water is from the same kind of turbines used in windmills, but this time the turbines are usually inside long tubes built into giant dams. When the water from the dam is released down the tubes the blades of the turbines are spun round really fast – the electricity they produce is called **hydroelectric energy**. Some other types of renewable energy come from the waves and tides in the sea, from burning wood and other fuels made from plants (**bioenergy**), and from places where the rocks underground are hot enough to make the steam to drive big electricity turbines (**geothermal energy**).

'Look at this light bulb,' says Henry, stepping into the hallway. 'As soon as I flick the switch it starts drawing electricity down the wires to our house. Miles away there's a big power station burning fossil fuels and producing carbon dioxide to create this electricity.'

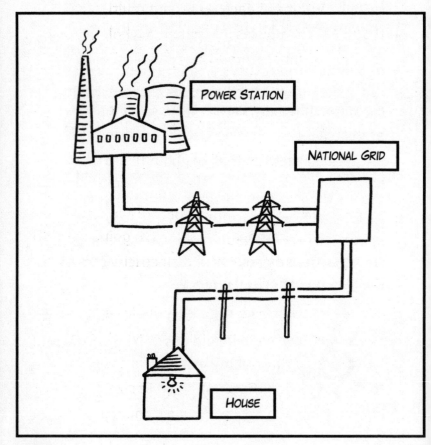

'Is it the same for TVs and stuff?' asks Max.

'Yes. Every time someone leaves on a light, a TV or anything else that uses electricity, the power station has to burn more fossil fuel and so more carbon dioxide gets released. One light on its own might only mean a few extra kilograms of each week, but multiply that by all the houses in a street, a whole town or an entire country and the masses of wasted electricity mean a huge amount of extra greenhouse gases get pumped into the atmosphere.'

'In that case, flick that switch off!' orders Max.

'I will!' says Henry. 'That's one of my ways to get a small carbon footprint – I'm going to seek and destroy any wasted electricity in our house.'

'So Flora's got her runoo-a-bubbles and you've got your seeking and destroying. Now I just need to think of my own brilliant way to cut my carbon footprint down to size. I know – what about Max Power? I could use

my super-strength to power things. Henry,
lend me your bike! If I can just hook it up to a
generator and pedal really fast, I'm sure I'll be

 98

able to create loads of electricity, especially if I eat a Chocolate Sundae beforehand. I'll have this global warming problem "licked" in no time!'

'Er . . . Max, I'm sure you're really powerful and everything, but I think even you might struggle to produce all the energy we need,' says Henry, switching on his computer. 'Let's see . . . OK, so you need about ten thousand units of electricity, called "watt hours", to supply the average house for one day. According to my computer you can generate about two-thirds of a "watt hour" for every Chocolate Sundae. So, by my reckoning, you'd need to eat about seventeen thousand Chocolate Sundaes every day to produce enough electricity for one house.'

Max looks put out (and a little green). 'So, none of my super-powers can solve global warming – not my super-strength, my super-speed, not even my super-chocolate-eating. We're doomed!'

Henry and Flora grin. 'It's not quite as bad

as all that. Your idea is still a good one and there are loads more things you can do. Let's get started and we'll show you just how easy it can be.'

CHAPTER
ELEVEN

They follow the red lights out of Henry's room and into the hall. One room is aglow with them. Max turns on the overhead light.

'Ha! I thought so!' says Henry. 'It's my big sister Fran again. She's out at the shops, and she's left everything on standby. See, you can tell by the humming noise everything's making. All this time this stuff's been wasting electricity from the power station and helping to cause more global warming.'

Max dives to the floor, rolls and switches off all the sockets, shouting, 'Maximus to the rescue!'

THOSE ARE STANDBY LIGHTS. EVEN WHEN YOU THINK YOU'VE TURNED SOMETHING OFF, IF THE LIGHT'S ON, THEN IT'S STILL USING ENERGY.

Standby killers

If you're at home, wait till everything is quiet and then concentrate. Listen very carefully and you'll probably just about be able to hear a hum. Over on the stereo a little red light gives the game away – that's standby power.

The energy being dispensed in our households through things being left on standby is a terrible waste. We see those little red or blue lights on our TVs, games consoles, set-top boxes and mobile phone chargers so often that it's all too easy to forget that they are slowly eating up vast amounts of energy. In Britain alone about 3,000,000 tonnes of carbon dioxide is produced every year by power stations just to produce all the electricity wasted by standby power. So keep those gadgets switched off!

Flora's facts

If everybody in the country stopped leaving their appliances on standby for one year, we would save enough electricity to power 100,000 homes for the next year.

Max, Henry and Flora continue their exploration of the house in their bid to cut down on electricity wastage.

'Henry! Someone's left a light on in the bathroom,' points out Max.

'I bet that was Fran again,' sighs Henry. 'Big sisters are the worst.'

'Let's turn it off then, and plug another electricity leak. This is easy!' announces Max. 'Hey, why are all your light bulbs curly?' he continues. 'They look weird.'

'Well,' explains Henry, 'they're special low-energy ones – they use up much less electricity than normal bulbs.'

'And we like them because they help FIGHT GLOBAL WARMING!' cries Max.

Light fantastic

Somewhere, lurking in the cloakroom, the spare bedroom or the hall, a light is on.

Hunt down those energy-wasters and turn them off. Well done. Now, what kind of bulb is it?

Fighting global warming can be so easy. Take something as simple as swapping an old-fashioned light bulb for a low-energy one. They're a bit more expensive, but they last for ages and they reduce your energy bills. Just one bulb can stop 60 kg of greenhouse gases – enough to fill a bedroom – getting into the atmosphere each year. Soon everybody will be using them.

'Another thing to look out for is overheating,'
says Henry. 'If the house is too hot, don't
just open a window – turn the heating down
instead.'

'But what if it's really cold in the house?'
asks Max.

'Don't turn the heating
up – put on a jumper, or, in
your case, an extra-thick
superhero cape. Let's
look at the list Miss
Weatherbottom
gave us.

Miss Weatherbottom's hot facts
for a cooler home

Computer

Screen savers aren't energy savers. Switch the monitor off while you're away from your desk and you'll halve the energy use of the computer. For computers that are in constant use, the energy-saving options can make quite a difference. The 'sleep mode' can cut greenhouse-gas emissions by 80 per cent – this is where you set your computer to drain less electricity when no one is using it. Of course there's an easy way to get the full 100 per cent cut: switch the computer off.

Games console

Guitar Hero may be great, but if you want to be the ultimate climate-change hero then hit that OFF switch whenever you've finished playing.

1

Heating

With central heating we can slop around our houses in shorts and a T-shirt as the snow piles up outside. We can then complain that it's too hot, pad barefoot across the carpet and open the window. Heating the average family home emits about four tonnes of greenhouse gas each year, but by pulling on a jumper and turning the heating down a notch or two we can give the boiler a break and stop hundreds of kilograms of greenhouse gases being poured into the atmosphere.

A lot of fossil fuel is burned to heat up the water in our homes and this means a lot of greenhouse gases are produced – just fixing a dripping hot-water tap can save more than 100 kg of greenhouse gases a year.

2

Stereos and TVs

Together, these quietly humming appliances are eating up electricity just to sit in standby mode. In the average house, three-quarters of a tonne of greenhouse gases are emitted every year by this route. On a national scale the wastage of energy and emission of greenhouse gases from standby power is simply embarrassing. In Australia, standby power is responsible for over 5,000,000 tonnes of greenhouse gases every year, and in the USA the figure is closer to 30,000,000 tonnes just to keep all those appliances humming.

Gadgets

After every Christmas countless tonnes of infrared binoculars, chocolate fountains and robot dogs lie forgotten in cupboards and drawers. Millions of batteries go into all these things, adding to the huge amounts of energy needed to make them in the first place. Try to avoid buying (or asking for) battery-operated items whenever possible. This can make a huge difference, and using rechargeable batteries instead of buying bucket-loads of new ones will help too.

In the kitchen

At some time, things do have to be replaced. Just one too many slices of jammy toast will get posted into the DVD player by your baby brother, the washing machine will start whining and belching smoke, and the fridge will start to smell even worse than Dad's blue cheese sandwiches. So, if you do find yourself being dragged along to the shops to buy a new kitchen appliance, remember this. Washing machines and the rest come with labels telling you how bad or good they are at saving energy. The labels vary from country to country with a star rating (the more stars the better) in the USA and Australia, and a letter rating in Europe. For letter ratings, A is the best (Ace), dropping to G (for Gruesome).

5

CHAPTER TWELVE

Max's stomach is rumbling. 'Henry, all this planet saving is making me hungry. I need to keep up my super-strength, you know! Please can we raid your fridge?'

'Sure! In fact, the kitchen's a great place to investigate global warming.'

'Brilliant. I fancy a burger.'

'Sorry, Max – can't help you there. Burgers come from cows, which aren't the most environmentally friendly of animals given all the methane they fart and burp. My family tries not to eat too much beef.'

Cow farts and bad breath

Get downwind of a herd of cows and your nose will quickly tell you that they smell. Along with that stink comes an awful lot of a powerful global warming gas called **methane**. Most of it is burped out, with the rest coming out as cow farts. Other animals like sheep produce methane too, but cows are the biggest belchers of the stuff at up to 500 litres per animal per day. Every beef steak results in around fifteen times its own weight of greenhouse-gas emissions even before you add in the transport emissions. Eating fewer burgers will help keep a lid on all that greenhouse gas. If you're a veggie, then give

yourself a pat on the back – as well as leading to lots of greenhouse gases, meat production uses many more resources like water.

While we're talking of methane farts and burps, sheep weigh in with about 30 litres of methane each per day, while pigs emit about 8 litres. And, yes, some humans can also release large volumes of methane, although thankfully the condition is quite rare. Whereas most of us let out just a few hundred millilitres in the privacy of our own bathrooms, some (probably quite lonely) souls emit as much as 3 litres of methane per day.

'I didn't know that food could be bad for the environment,' ponders Max.

'Yep, 'fraid so,' says Henry. 'It's also a problem when food has to travel on planes, trucks and boats for thousands of miles before reaching us. The further our food has to travel the more fossil fuels are burned moving it around and the more greenhouse gases are produced. These "food miles", as well as the growing and storage of all our food, can add to the global warming problem.'

'Is there anything in your fridge which isn't a menace?' asks Max.

'Of course. Why don't you take the Fridge Challenge to find out? There's a fudge sundae in it if you win . . .'

'A fudge sundae? I'm in! Er . . . what do I have to do exactly?'

Take the Fridge Challenge

Go to your fridge and randomly take out four things. Now check their 'Country of Origin' labels.

For every item that's from your own country, give yourself one point. If it's from abroad, take one point away.

RESULTS:
Points −4 to −2: That's one well-travelled bunch of food, and it's probably added a lot of greenhouse gases to the atmosphere on its journey to your fridge.

Points –1 to 1: Not bad, but could you do better? Some types of food have to be brought in from abroad, but many can be bought from local markets or even grown at home.

Points 2 to 4: Great stuff. That's some really cool food. To make even more impact, stick to food that's in season – like apples in the autumn and strawberries in the summer.

'Right Max. What have you got?' Henry asks.

Max's head emerges from the fridge, with chocolate round his mouth. 'I've got an egg, a lettuce, some strawberries . . . and a fudge sundae,' he says. 'I might have already eaten some of the sundae.'

'Good work – you've won maximum points! All those items were either made in this country or grown in our back garden. Which means you've won the sundae!'

Seconds later, Max has eaten the whole thing. 'Mmm, that was lovely,' he sighs. 'Where's the bin, Henry?'

Flora points at the recycling bin. 'You'll be wanting the recycling bin for that wrapper, as it's made from cardboard. Gotta remember the three Rs!' she says.

Max looks blank.

'REDUCE, REUSE and RECYCLE. Each R is a great weapon to use against global warming. REDUCE basically means buying less stuff – a lot of food gets wasted because we buy too much of it. REUSE is doing things like using the same plastic bag lots of times instead of having lots of plastic bags that you only use once, and RECYCLE – well, that's what you're going to do now.'

Max looks puzzled. 'So putting this wrapper in a different bin will help fight global warming?' he asks. 'I don't understand.'

'It means that next time someone makes a box for another fudge sundae they don't have to chop down a tree and mash it up to make another cardboard wrapper,' says Flora. 'They can just make new boxes out of the old ones which have been put in the recycling bin. It saves on trees, saves on energy and so helps keep the world a little cooler. Come on, let's go over to my garden and I'll show you how it's done!'

Flora's facts

The average item of food you buy in the supermarket has travelled further than the length of the UK to get there.

Henry Hutchinson

Describe the recycling process for the packaging of a product you eat regularly

A week in the life of a fudge-sundae box

Sunday Have just arrived at the supermarket and they've put me and the other boxes of fudge sundaes on a brightly lit shelf. I hope someone comes along and buys us soon — the music they play in this shop is awful!

Monday This is it. Someone has just bought me and my fudge sundae. Travelling home with lots of other shopping now.

Tuesday Spent a chilly night in a fridge. Wonder when someone will get around to eating this fudge sundae. Hang on, I think someone's coming . . .

Wednesday Well, a smiling man with a cape and special goggles ate the sundae and then put me in a large bin with lots of other cardboard. It's nice to be out of that fridge.

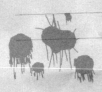

Thursday I've never seen so many boxes! Today some men collected me and all the other cardboard and took us to a factory full of mountains of boxes. They've put me in a heap labelled 'rolls'. Wonder if I'm going to be made into a sandwich box.

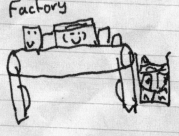

Friday That was all a bit soggy. They soaked me in water and mixed me up with the other boxes. Now we've been dried and rolled into new sheets of cardboard ready for making into something new. Still don't know what I'll be though.

Saturday Hmm, turns out I'm not a box for a sundae or a sandwich. This time I'm a toilet roll!

A

very inventive, Henry! What a journey!

Recycling

Instead of having to produce everything we use from scratch, recycling means a huge amount of materials and energy can be saved. From cans and bottles to paper and cardboard, every item you recycle rather than throw in the bin is a stab in the side of global warming. Avoiding stuff with too much packaging, buying more loose fruit and veg and checking the logos on packaging to see if it's recyclable will all help give the bin a break.

Flora's facts

An average wheely bin gathers about 20 kg of rubbish every week. In other words, over a year, each of us ditches ten times our own weight in rubbish!

CHAPTER THIRTEEN

'Those garbage munchers seem pretty handy,' says Max. 'But what do you do with all the worm poo?'

'The worm poo is the best bit!' replies Flora. 'They turn all that kitchen waste into the best compost ever. The plants love it and some of the vegetables grow massive!'

'Giant vegetables?' thinks Max.

'Yes, look at this – it's my prize pumpkin for Halloween,' says Flora. 'And it's all thanks to worm poo made from kitchen rubbish!'

Flora's facts

About 60 per cent of the stuff we throw away could actually be used for compost.

Worms

No global warming warrior should be without his worms. They may be small but these wriggly guys pack a serious climate change punch. In your compost heap they'll speed up the conversion of garden waste to compost. In a worm farm they can happily chew their way through all the uncooked vegetable waste, banana skins and apple cores from the kitchen. They'll also turn eggshells, tea bags and even dog hair into top-grade compost! For every kilogram of potato peelings, tea bags or grass clippings that you compost rather than send off to landfill (big holes in the ground where a lot of our rubbish is buried), you'll stop around two kilograms of greenhouse gas from going into the atmosphere. This is because landfill sites produce loads of the greenhouse gas **methane** (the same stuff that's in cow burps and farts).Over a year, the average household can shave almost a tonne off their emissions in this way. Not bad work for a few worms.

Compost

Lovely stuff, this – the ultimate in recycling. Take a load of stinky waste from the garden (old flower heads and lawn trimmings), put it on the compost heap and keep it well mixed up and, after a few months, you get lovely rich compost with which to grow prize-winning vegetables free of charge. Composting works by worms, bacteria and fungi eating the garden waste and breaking it down into the crumbly black stuff that plants like so much. Even better, composting garden waste means it doesn't end up in the local landfill site.

Home-grown food

Because it doesn't have to travel very far to get to your dinner plate, any food you grow at school or at home means you avoid all those climate-warming food miles that come with food flown or trucked to the shops from abroad. If you can get Mum and Dad to give you a bit of garden to grow things in, then brilliant. No garden? No problem. Ask your teacher whether you can grow vegetables at school.

'Well, I'm certainly learning a lot of ways to fight global warming,' says Max. 'I think I know what to put in my carbon footprint picture now: saving energy at home, remembering to Reduce, Reuse and Recycle, growing some of my own food, composting . . .'

'That's a great start, Max,' says Henry, 'but we've got loads more ideas for you. Have you seen Flora's big butts?'

Max creases up with laughter. 'Butts . . . big butts . . . hee hee hee!'

Flora points to two large containers by the wall. 'WATER butts, Max!' she scowls. 'They collect rain from the roof of the house and garage. Tap water has to be purified to make it safe to drink, and this process uses up energy and leads to more planet-warming emissions. But the stuff we collect in the water butts is great for the plants, it's free and it's good for the planet.'

'Great. I'll go and get one from a shop. I'll ask for the biggest butt they have!' Max announces.

Henry and Flora roll their eyes. 'Very funny, Max!'

Henry Hutchinson

Describe how you would grow your favourite fruit or vegetable.

1. Put a few stones at the bottom of a plant pot so that the water can drain out.

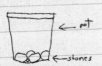
← pot
← stones

2. Fill the pot with soil.

soil

3. Press a few tomato seeds into the soil, a fingerwidth apart.

tomato seeds

4. Cover the seeds with more soil.

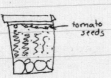

5. Place the pot on a windowsill where it will get lots of light.

6. When the seeds start to grow, pick out a few so that only the healthiest are left.

7. As the seeds get bigger, plant them into larger pots.

8. Enjoy your big pile of tomatoes!

A

Tomatoes, Henry, or tomato ketchup? Let me know if they grow . . .

135

Alien invasion

Gardens are in the front line when it comes to climate change. We can nip inside if it gets too hot or wet but the plants and animals outside just have to put up with it. As the climate changes, new plants and animals will spread to new areas – these are called 'aliens'. Some might be useful, like new types of crop for farmers to grow, but others will definitely be bad aliens. Some weeds, pests and diseases are already spreading to new places because of climate change, while some of the plants that we're used to – like the lush grass in our lawns – will find it harder and harder to cope as summers get hotter and drier.

A great way to help the animals that are being put at risk by climate change is to provide shelter and food for them in your garden – things like berry bushes and foxgloves to feed the birds and bees, and log piles and beetle boxes for hedgehogs and insects to live in. If there's no room at home, then school gardens can be perfect for all this.

CHAPTER FOURTEEN

The next day Max meets Henry and Flora on the walk to school.

'Morning, climate champions! I guess walking doesn't cause global warming then?'

'No – it's all those cars and trucks over there that are the problem,' says Henry. 'The worst ones are the really big ones. Some of them chuck out more than ten tonnes of greenhouse gases a year.'

'I suppose people have to get to work and school though – and sometimes it's too far to walk,' says Max.

'Yes,' says Flora, 'but most of these cars only go a few miles and hardly anyone doubles up on passengers. Look, there's Gripper in his mum's massive

car. And he lives closer to school than we do.'

'He does say he'd like to walk, but his mum thinks it's too dangerous because of all the traffic.'

'Wait – so kids are taken to school in cars because there are too many cars on the way to school? My head is beginning to hurt again!' exclaims Max.

'I know. It doesn't make sense to us either,' says Flora.

'Anyway, I can't wait to show Miss Weatherbottom my picture – you two have given me loads of great ideas!'

'No problem, Max,' says Henry. 'Flora was just saying how we could do a special letter for you to give to the President too.'

'Brilliant. As soon as Climate Club is over I'll go and see him,' Max announces.

The school run

Every weekday, rain or shine, it's off to school.
It may only be a short distance but if you travel
in Mum and Dad's gas-guzzling car to and from
school each day, the contribution it makes to
global warming can soon pile up.

Car

Short of flying to school it doesn't get much
worse than this. If taking the school bus, cycling
or walking aren't possible, then you might be
able to car-share. This is where parents take it in
turns to drive a group of school friends to school
all together. It can really help reduce the global-
warming impact of the school run.

Bus

OK, so some of your classmates smell, but it's
got to be better than having to listen to Dad's
favourite music on his car stereo every morning.
Catch the bus and strike a blow against global
warming.

Bike or walk

Travel greenhouse-gas-free to school and back. More and more schools are now organizing schemes like 'Park and Stride', 'The Golden Boot' and 'The Walking School Bus', where you join all your friends on the walk in to school, picking up more and more people as you go. A teacher or parent walks at the front as the 'driver' and another one walks at the back to keep everyone safe.

Flora's facts

One double-decker bus holds the same number of people as twenty full cars, but takes up seven times less space on the road.

Later that day, Max, Henry and Flora are sitting in class, waiting for Miss Weatherbottom to announce the winner of the carbon footprint competition. Gripper is bragging to them.

'Well, I hope you're all ready to lose,' he sneers. 'I've got the best ever anti-global-warming invention – look!'

'So what is it?' asks Flora. 'Your house looks pretty bad for global warming to me. It's got TVs and gadgets on everywhere – it must be wasting loads of electricity.'

'Yeah, it is,' replies Gripper. 'I decided not to waste any time with all that energy-saving stuff. Check out the other side of my picture for my invention that will save us all. I present to you . . . Gripper's Gust-o-matic!'

Gripper turns over his picture. The other side shows him grinning widely with two battery fans attached to his belt and pointing up at right angles, blowing air at his armpits.

'See! With Gripper's Gust-o-matic no one will need to use deodorants any more and so

142

the ozone layer will be saved! Told you I'd win.'

Er . . . I'm sorry to have to tell you, Gripper,' says Flora, 'but the ozone layer is different from climate change. And judging by how you smell, I think you should probably go back to using deodorant!'

The ozone 'hole'

Ozone is a gas that is mostly found high in the Earth's atmosphere. It protects us from the most harmful rays that come from the Sun, called ultraviolet rays. In the past deodorant sprays used to produce gases that destroyed the ozone in the atmosphere, and so allowed more of the dangerous ultraviolet rays to get through – this is called the ozone hole. To stop the ozone layer getting any thinner it was agreed that deodorants wouldn't use the damaging gases in their sprays any more and it now looks as though the thin bits will eventually thicken up again. So it's best to think of the ozone layer as something completely different from global warming and climate change, though many people still get them mixed up.

'Huh!' says Gripper sulkily.

'I stuck with my "seek and destroy" electricity hunt for my competition entry,' says Henry. 'Look.'

'It's good, but mine's definitely
the best,' boasts Max. 'Look.'

'You see, I worked out that all the melting water around my ice cave can power an electricity turbine, and then my Max power bike can give me some extra electricity for the lights,' he explains. 'When I'm riding it I keep warm AND

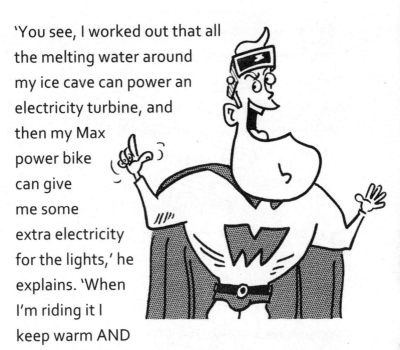

all the carbon dioxide I breathe out goes along to my greenhouse. The vegetables will love it and will grow huge! I'm jealous of your worm farm though, Flora. I tried every shop I could to get one last night, but they had all sold out. I really wanted my own army of wormy composters!'

Miss Weatherbottom examines each of the pictures very carefully then claps her hands.

'Well, Climate Champions,' she says,

'you've all done very well. Gripper, I'm afraid your invention wasn't quite what we needed, but well done for trying so hard. It was difficult to decide on a winner but, for his clever use of plants to use up the carbon dioxide he breathes out, the top prize goes to . . . Max!'

Everyone cheers.

'Thank you, everyone,' says Max, blushing, 'and especially Henry and Flora. Er . . . what's the prize?'

'It's your very own worm farm, Max!' says Miss Weatherbottom with a smile. 'Just what you always wanted, I'm sure!'

Max, Henry and Flora are putting the worms into their new home ready for Max to fly them to his ice cave.

'Well, they look pretty happy,' says Flora. 'Now let's finish our special guide for the President, Max. We're going to call it "Whacking Global Warming in a Weekend". Do you want to add anything?'

Flora is scribbling furiously. 'Brilliant!' she says. 'I'll sign it "Max, Henry and Flora – Climate Champions".'

WHACKING GLOBAL WARMING IN A WEEKEND

Dear Mr President,

Global warming is caused by special heat-trapping gases called greenhouse gases. The more we burn fossil fuels like coal and oil, the more greenhouse gas there is in the air and the warmer the planet gets. More warming causes changes in weather patterns all over the world and this is called climate change. Climate change is threatening millions of people with things like droughts, heatwaves and flooding. So you need to do something. Quick. Here's how to start:

1. Replace all light bulbs with low-energy ones.
2. Hunt down lights that have been left on and turn them off.
3. Kill off standby power wastage by TVs and other gadgets.

4. Travel less by car. Walk and cycle more instead.

5. Swap the gas-guzzling big car for one with a smaller engine.

6. Fly less (unless you're Max). Use the train, and holiday closer to home.

7. Remember the three Rs: Reduce, Reuse, Recycle.

8. Avoid buying too much meat and food that has travelled a long way.

9. Compost rubbish from the kitchen and garden, and get yourself a big butt (for collecting rainwater!).

10. Turn down the heating and pull on a jumper (or extra-thick cape if you're a superhero).

11. Get the garden at home or school growing monster veg. with plenty of worm poo.

12. Tell your friends and family all about climate change and what they can do to help fight it.

When you've done all that you can get on with some of the big President stuff too:

1. Help protect all the people already in danger from the extra flooding, drought, heatwaves and hunger caused by climate change.

2. Make sure more electricity and heating comes from renewable energy sources like the wind, the seas and the sun.

3. Give more protection to the tropical forests.

4. Make all power stations capture and store the greenhouse gases they produce.

5. Provide more climate-friendly ways for people to get around, like good cycle paths and bus networks.

6. Make sure that the best climate-saving inventions in the rich countries are given to the poorer countries, so they can become richer without making the same planet-warming mistakes we made.

by MAX, HENRY and FLORA
CLIMATE CHANGE CHAMPIONS

Max is all ready to go.

'Well, better get these worms home and then it's off to the President's house – I've got a lot to tell him,' he says.

'I hope you can come back soon, Max,' says Flora. 'Miss Weatherbottom wants me and Henry to show the other kids in school how to fight climate change too! We're going to set up recycling bins in every classroom, appoint Energy Monitors to make sure lights and things are off when they're not being used, and next week we start our first "walking school bus" – even Gripper is going to join in.'

'That's fantastic. I'll tell Mr President we've started fighting climate change here, but that he and every person in every country needs to help. Goodbye! I'll be back soon for Climate Club!'

Climate change goes to school

When your teachers have recovered from hearing about all the ways you've tackled climate change at home you can hit them with all the ways it can be tackled at school too. If Henry and Flora can make a difference, then imagine what a whole class of Henrys and Floras could do. Try this Climate Champion's Hit List:

⚡ **Lights out** There are loads of lights in a school and many are left on even when no one is in the room, especially in the washrooms. Try hunting these energy-wasters down and switching them off.

⚡ **Does not compute** Computer monitors don't have to be on all the time – seek out the ones that aren't being used and make sure they're turned off.

⚡ **My brain is melting** Is school just too hot? Check that the classroom heating isn't set too high.

⚡ **Drip dry** Wasted water from taps that are left on is bad enough, but if it's hot water then its like pouring energy down the drain – seek them out and turn them off.

⚡ **Teach your teachers the three Rs** Most schools get through an awful lot of paper and this can mean a lot of trees being cut down and mashed up. REDUCE how much is used by using both sides of each sheet and making sure anything from the school printer or photocopier is printed on both sides. REUSE old paper that has a blank side whenever you can. RECYCLE not just paper, but metal cans, plastic and glass too.

⚡ **Banana-skin bonanza** No school of climate champions should be without a compost bin for old fruit and vegetables. If your teacher's brave enough, you could even suggest a school worm farm!

⚡ **Global gardening** With bird boxes and fruit bushes the school garden can be made into a refuge for birds trying to find food and shelter in a changing climate. Even better, if there's somewhere to grow vegetables then school dinners might improve too!

⚡ **Club together** Does your school have a Climate Change club? If not, why not start one and be its president?

⚡ **Sign of the times** A global warming warrior can't be everywhere at once. Break out the recycled paper and make some magnificent posters to tell everyone else in the school how they can help.

⚡ **My bus has no wheels** Walking to school is a great way to fight global warming, and if it's in a 'walking bus' it can be safer and more fun too.

⚡ **My school is a power station** Some schools have already got wind turbines or solar panels to help provide their electricity. Why not yours?

⚡ **Heads will roll** Head teachers should love all climate champions – after all, you'll save the school lots of money! Ask them if the school has a climate change plan. If it doesn't, then help them make one.

Why is SNOT green?

The First Science Museum Question and Answer Book

Glenn Murphy

Why is snot green? Do rabbits fart? What is space made of? Where does all the water go at low tide? Can animals talk? What are scabs for? Will computers ever be cleverer than people?

Discover the answers to these and an awful lot of other brilliant questions frequently asked at the Science Museum in this wonderfully funny and informative book.

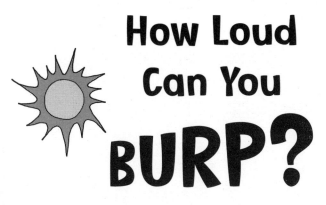

How Loud Can You BURP?

and other extremely important questions
(and answers) from the Science Museum

Glenn Murphy

How loud can you burp? Could we use animal poo in
power stations to make electricity? Why is water wet,
and is anything wetter than water? What's the deadliest
disease in the world? What are clouds for?

A second volume of questions and answers from the
Science Museum by the author of the mega-bestselling
WHY IS SNOT GREEN? A wonderfully funny and
informative book with loads of fascinating facts and no
boring bits!

Stuff that scares your PANTS off!

**The Science Museum Book of Scary Things
(and ways to avoid them)**

Glenn Murphy

What scares you most? Spiders or sharks? Ghosts or aliens? Dentists or darkness?

This amazing book takes apart your deepest, darkest fears. With a bit of biology, a spot of psychology and oodles of lovely facts and figures, you'll learn everything there is to know about the stuff that scares your pants off.

Once you've read this book, you will be able to look terror in the eye and make it run away whimpering. You might even want to change your middle name to 'danger'!

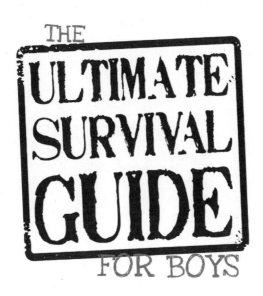

Mike Flynn

This book will teach you everything you need to know to
survive in the wilderness (or your back garden!)

Learn how to navigate by the stars, read a map, use a
compass, build a shelter, signal for help, find water, leave
tracking signs for others to follow and put together the
essential survival kit.

Take inspiration from the experts – find out how the SAS
approaches survival, how the Bedouin get by with barely
any water and how the Vikings used to navigate.

Read this book and you'll be prepared for
any eventuality!

DO THIS AT HOME! TRY AT HOME!

28 spectacular experiments for scientists of all ages

Explosions possible
Mess likely
Fun guaranteed!

Here at Punk Science HQ we just love doing experiments! So join us as we show you how to:

- use a lemon to power a light
- make a fizz bang rocket
- create a working submarine

And much, much more . . .

With a free DVD of extra experiments that you definitely CAN'T do at home!

A selected list of titles available from Macmillan Children's Books

The prices shown below are correct at the time of going to press. However, Macmillan Publishers reserves the right to show new retail prices on covers, which may differ from those previously advertised.

Why Is Snot Green? Glenn Murphy	978-0-330-44852-9	£4.99
How Loud Can You Burp? Glenn Murphy	978-0-330-45409-4	£4.99
Stuff That Scares Your Pants Off! Glenn Murphy	978-0-330-47724-6	£4.99
Do Try This At Home! Punk Science	978-0-230-70741-2	£12.99
The Ultimate Survival Guide for Boys Mike Flynn	978-0-230-70051-2	£9.99

All Pan Macmillan titles can be ordered from our website, www.panmacmillan.com, or from your local bookshop and are also available by post from:

Bookpost, PO Box 29, Douglas, Isle of Man IM99 1BQ

Credit cards accepted. For details:
Telephone: 01624 677237
Fax: 01624 670923
Email: bookshop@enterprise.net
www.bookpost.co.uk

Free postage and packing in the United Kingdom